How to Invest Now and RETIRE RICH

How to Invest Now and RETIRE RICH

David L. Markstein

AN ARC BOOK

ARCO PUBLISHING COMPANY, INC.
219 Park Avenue South, New York, N.Y. 10003

Portions of this book first appeared
as a series of articles in *Dynamic
Maturity,* a magazine published by
the American Association of Retired
Persons

Published by ARCO PUBLISHING COMPANY, Inc.
219 Park Avenue South, New York, N.Y. 10003

Library of Congress Catalog Card Number 72-95275
ISBN 0-668-02930-7

Printed in the United States of America

For Ruz and Darrell

CONTENTS

1. The Policy to Pursue Before You Retire   1
2. The World of the Stock Certificate   6
3. The Big Play in Foreign Stocks   11
4. Some Little-Known Ways to Build Capital   17
5. The Fortunes in Grain and Metal   27
6. Capital Gains from Run-Down Houses   33
7. Making Money from Land   39
8. Real Estate Investing the "REIT" Way   48
9. Bonds for Big Money Gains   53
10. How to Avoid Tax on Investment Income   59
11. The Money in Mutual Funds   64
12. How Stock Market Changes Can Make You Rich   70
13. Count on More Inflation   76
14. After Retirement—A High Income for Life   81

Chapter One

THE POLICY TO PURSUE BEFORE
YOU RETIRE

The problem is to obtain high income after retirement; the solution begins before you symbolically or actually receive your gold watch and handshake and set out into a world where there is no more work.

Whenever the word "retirement" comes up, I evoke an image of people who trustfully planned years ago for a retirement world in which a seaside cottage rented for $75 a month, steak in a restaurant cost $2, and a nickel bought you the morning paper. That world succumbed to inflation. Now the cottage costs $250 a month, the restaurant sirloin $8 to $10 a serving, and the nickel newspaper anywhere from a dime to a quarter. *The $250 cottage, $10 steak and 15¢ newspaper won't last either.*

By the time actual retirement comes, these may be as much a wistful dream as the cottage, steak, and newspaper of ten years ago. It is necessary to plan for a world in which today's costs will be the good old prices and tomorrow's will be somewhere up in the economic sky. No reason why that should scare you, however.

I say invest for growth—conservatively, of course—then the transition into a world in which you draw extra income to overcome inflationary bite won't scare you.

Q. This threat of a continued inflation is frightening. Isn't the government doing something about it? Won't this spiral of higher and higher prices ever stop? Our retirement isn't going to be ruined that way—or is it?

A. You bet inflation will continue. If you don't bet on it, you are likely to find those happy later years reduced to penny-pinching and making do. It's possible to make retirement an affluent, economically easy time for you. But only if you bet—and heavily—on continued inflation.

Q. You are probably right about continuation of inflation. It appears that we have to think about two kinds of climate. The kind made by the temperature and the sun won't be there unless we also think in terms of the climate for our dollars. How can we make the sun shine on them so they will grow?

A. As I see it, planning for an affluent retirement breaks into two phases with a slower, smaller transition between them. In the first phase, we try for growth. Not the very rapid growth of the sort exemplified by what were called the go-go stocks in 1968 (in 1969 and 1970, those went-went). Say you have $20,000 cash capital. If this should be lost by trying too hard in go-go stocks, or in any other way of attempting to make it in a big hurry, then such a stake is not easily replaced. We will look for growth, but not necessarily rapid growth.

Later on, we'll institute good income-producing investments. With those, too, we'll try for gradual growth —this time of income itself—so that inflation during your retirement years won't render those years progressively more strapped and increasingly less pleasurable.

We'll transition slowly between those two phases. A quick switchover might be unadvisable.

Q. You mention a slow transition as retirement age approaches. Wouldn't it be better to get all the growth we can right up to retirement itself? That way, we might achieve larger capital on which to earn income.

A. The soundest way to get somewhere quickly is not always the fast way. Your capital consists of more than merely cash in the bank. There is the value of your home, for example, long paid for and worth many times what you paid. On retirement, you may want to move to a sunny climate. Will you be able to sell that house in a hurry? Do you know what you wish to accomplish with proceeds of such a sale? Will you buy a new home elsewhere? Invest the money? Use part for a condominium purchase, part to produce income? Such decisions should be accomplished slowly.

Not all growth-type investments you can make would be as easily sold as stocks and mutual funds. We should think in terms of one or more of the following growth vehicles:

- Stocks of good corporations with growth potential.
- Mutual funds aimed at capital appreciation (but not necessarily at in-out stock market trading to produce it; such funds tend to be winners one year, losers the next).
- Real estate with good, growing rentals.
- The remodel-resell property market in which you can sometimes find run-down houses at distress prices, remodel to the level of the neighborhood, and resell at a capital gain.
- Participation in petroleum drilling and production, in citrus groves, or cattle raising. In these, there is tax shelter in addition to growth potential.

With $20,000 available, you should not spread yourself thinly among all of these. But all should be considered. Next, you should develop a statement of net worth.

Q. What is net worth?

A. A balance sheet, or net worth statement, tells how much you own, free and clear of debt and encumbrance.

In one column, list everything you own: home, cash, paid-up insurance policies, any debts owed to you—the works. Head the list "assets."

Call the next column "liabilities." In it put down long-term debt, if any, accounts you owe to stores and the like, contingent debts (as, for example, a cosigned note), and other things you owe or which detract from your list of assets.

Total the numbers in each list. Subtract the smaller —in your case, hopefully, the liabilities are less—from the larger. The result is your net worth.

Points to Remember

1. You don't reach retirement age in a single leap, and you should not expect to reslant your financial affairs to retirement living all at once. In order to retire rich, planning should begin well in advance of actual withdrawal from the work force and hopeful removal to a sun climate and a life where everything can be fun—if there are sufficient funds to pay for it.

2. Inflation is a fact of life. There are sound reasons to expect that it will continue. The welfare-war state gobbles tax dollars so fast that deficit spending is a way of doing things in Washington. Add the inflationary impact of higher wages and costs to the dollar growth forced by deficit spending, and you have a near-guarantee that tomorrow's prices will be considerably above today's.

3. Planning for richer retirement must face this fact. At first, emphasis in financial planning should be on capital growth, changing slowly rather than suddenly to emphasis on production of high retirement income.

4. Your plan for the days when you'll go out of the game to sit happily on the bench while another player takes over the work must look at the total money picture—stocks, bonds, real estate (home included), etc.

5. In succeeding chapters we will examine how to do this and will look additionally at tax-exempt and tax-sheltered investments, which permit accumulation of funds that the tax collector can't touch.

Chapter Two

THE WORLD OF THE STOCK CERTIFICATE

One of my clients once said to me: "The 1969–70 decline in stock markets wasn't just *a* bear market—it was a real Papa Bear." He was right. The big decline lasted longer than any since the disaster of the thirties; it went deeper in percentage of drop in average stock prices, and it was the first bear market since the doleful days of the thirties to go lower than the bottom of the bear market before it.

It *was* a Papa Bear.

Yet despite that large decline in stock prices, stocks still constitute a primary medium of investment for affluent retirement, and a primary means for keeping income abreast of inflation after retirement. Barring any calamity which would bring the United States and our whole way of life to an end—an inconceivable thought —stocks can always be expected to come back after the bear markets.

Q. What are stocks? Where do they differ from bonds, debentures, warrants, puts, calls, preferreds, and other kinds of securities?

A. Stocks represent ownership of a corporation. If you have 100 shares of the stock of corporation A and there are 1,000,000 shares outstanding, you are the owner of 1/10,000 of the company. Stocks' *earnings* are the amount of profit left after all costs, divided by the number of shares. Stocks pay *dividends* out of such earnings. The typical corporation might pay 50 to 70 percent of earnings in dividends, using the rest to generate future growth. Sometimes, a company husbands all of its earnings for plow-back. That is especially true of new, young corporations in growth areas. Thus, the dividends you receive from stocks are not guaranteed, nor are they necessarily the same from year to year. In a sound and growing company, they should increase steadily, but there is no warranty in any stock that this will happen, and dividend cuts have occurred in stocks of even the biggest, most basic corporations.

Bonds are different from stocks. A bond is a corporation's IOU. Unlike the debt note of an individual, a bond is negotiable. Instead of dividends from earnings, bonds pay *interest*, set at the time of issuance. Although cases of interest default have happened, this is rare, especially in bonds of the biggest companies. Bonds start out at *par*, the value (generally $1,000, sometimes $100, per bond) at which they are first sold and for which they will be redeemed when maturity date comes. Bond prices fluctuate. A few years ago, leading corporations could raise money at 3 percent. Now they sometimes have to pay 7 and 8 percent. As a result, investors no longer pay par for 3-percent bonds; these sell down to a price at which they return the 8 percent which is a going rate. So you buy a bond at the interest yield prevailing at the time of purchase. Interest payments do not fluctuate as do stock dividends. There is less danger, but no growth in income.

Debentures are a variety of unsecured bond. Warrants, puts, and calls are options to buy stock at a predetermined price. They are for use of speculators, not long-term investors and should never be used by investors looking for secure, affluent retirement. Preferred stock is a hybrid security; preferreds receive set yields as do bonds. They have less protection than bonds since bond-holders can (in theory but seldom in practice) force the sale of a company's assets to secure their income. Pre-ferred stockholders' dividends are generally higher than bond interest and must be paid before money can be disbursed to common stockholders.

Q. Explain blue-chip and speculative stocks.

A. In poker the blue chips are always assigned highest value. It is so in the stock market, where blue-chip stocks are those of the biggest, soundest, most solid com-panies. General Motors stock would be a blue chip. General Moontrotters would not—in fact, it would be considered highly speculative because (if there really were a company of this name) it would be engaged in a venture the outcome of which was in doubt. Most speculative stocks are like General Moontrotters. Often, too, they lack the vast financial underpinnings of a Gen-eral Motors, which is able to survive disasters and set-backs that might wreck a company of slender resources. However, greater growth potential often exists in smaller, more speculative stocks.

Q. Should the average person approaching retirement buy blue chips or try for the greater growth potential in speculative stocks?

A. That is a matter for personal preference, and your own psychology should be taken into account. Do you like to take chances? Can you watch things go wrong with a speculative stock and still sleep soundly? If so, then a portion of your retirement capital could be put into a package of two or three speculative stocks. But keep most of it in the blue chips.

As a general rule, stay with the sounder stocks.

Q. What criteria do you suggest for choosing stocks?

A. Go back to that earnings figure we mentioned earlier. Your first criterion should be that the company's earnings not fluctuate wildly. These should be fairly steady from year to year and they should increase, not necessarily spectacularly, but regularly. Without such continuing growth in earnings, there is no ability to pay increasing dividends that will be needed to save you from losing out to inflation, which is sure to continue in the future.

Next look for companies in sound fields. Steel is basic to our economy, but steelmakers' earnings frequently fluctuate. Automobiles are also basic, and auto makers' earnings fluctuate, but not to so great a degree; moreover, their earnings have tended in the past to increase over the longer period. Utilities, banks, and the like are an ultraconservative, yet growing, field.

Look for sound financial structure, expressed in a favorable ratio of assets to debts. A company short on cash might have to resort to financing at unfavorable times; therefore, cash position can be important to conservative growth.

Q. After we find the right stock, should we put it away and pay no further attention to market price, etc.?

A. By no means. Investing is not a static art. Fortunes of industries and companies change. The manufacture of buggies was once one of America's basic industries. Even within industries which have not gone down the road to nowhere as did the buggy industry, companies rise or drop back. You have only to look at Studebaker, Reo, or Nash in the automobile industry to see the importance of keeping pace with change. When a company's products seem to be on the side of obsolescence or decline, then bid goodbye to its stock or you will go down that road to nowhere.

Points to Remember

1. Despite ups and downs of stock prices—1969 and part of 1970 saw a very long and large down period—stocks in general tend to come back, and it has been a further tendency of stock prices in the past to go up faster than the dwindling dollar goes down in purchasing power.

2. The search for growth investments can center on either speculative, risky, but hopefully fast-growing younger companies; or on sounder, older, but slower-moving blue-chip stocks. Your own financial setup and the kind of person you are—whether you can sleep soundly while undergoing risk—should govern a choice of which type is for you.

3. Stocks, bonds, warrants, and preferreds are all securities but are not all alike any more than alley cats and elephants, both quadrupeds, are similar in more than the most basic respects. You must study securities to know what you're buying and how each type might fit your retirement package.

4. Even within a group, some securities represent more or less risk than others. The term "blue chip" in Wall Street refers to high quality and (usually) lessened risk of loss.

5. Statistics on company operation are widely published and can be secured through brokerage offices and libraries. Study these; do not invest blindly.

6. Investment is no static art. Despite folklore which holds that great fortunes can be accumulated by purchasing stocks, putting them away, and never selling, the fact is that this happens only to lucky people. Company and industry fortunes wax and wane. Buggies were once a great American industry. So, later, were railroads. You must be ready to change retirement investments with changing business times.

Chapter Three
THE BIG PLAY IN FOREIGN STOCKS

On August 17, 1971, the Dow Jones Industrial Average, by which most investors measure progress or decline of United States stocks in general, stood at 899.90. One year later to the day, the same Dow average was at 961.39. The gain of 61.49 points in a year was better upside performance than the Dow is able to make in most twelve-month periods. It represented a "profit" of 6.9 percent, assuming an investor had been able to buy the intangible average rather than a more tangible individual stock.

During the same hot week of August, 1971, an average of West German stocks stood at 103.98. The comparable index of Japanese stocks showed 2,283.88. A year later, investors sweltering in the August weather of 1972 were able to observe a reading of 118.44 on the West German index and 4,014.35 on the Japanese. On average, as expressed by these two indexes, West German securities had advanced 14.46 points, or 13.9 percent—double the profit rung up by the Dow Jones average of American stock prices. The Japanese performance was spectacular. It showed 1,730.47 points "profit"—a 76-percent advance in a single year.

There is a point to this discussion of statistics, percentages, and the performances of stock indexes of different nations. The point is that money is to be made, under the right conditions and at the right times, in

11

stocks of nations outside North America. At times these stocks show the kind of handsome profits capable of tripling an investor's money before he arrives at retirement age.

Q. Can an American invest this way, or does he have to be resident in Japan, Germany, or wherever?

A. The events, growth, and opportunity may be overseas, but you can participate right from the U.S.A.—just by picking up your telephone. You order foreign securities—provided they're in the right forms—as easily as you would order shares of General Motors and American Telephone, or mutual fund participations in Massachusetts Investors Trust or the Nicholas Strong Fund.

Q. Do foreign stock averages always perform better than American indexes?

A. By no means. But every dog has his day, and—no disrespect intended—so does every nation. Growth happens in different places at different times.

Earlier, we cited the performances of Japanese and West German stock averages during one twelve-month period. It is a paradox of twentieth-century history that the two defeated nations of World War II—laid low by bombing and kept down by extended occupation, with their cities in ruins, their productive capacities a shambles, and their people decimated and cowed by the manner as well as the awesome extent of their defeats—should have risen by the 1970s to be the two fastest-growing advanced countries. Some underdeveloped lands may have made better percentage progress. However, when measuring percentage gains from a low start, it is well to remember the words of a humble-hitting major league pitcher during the year when Roger Maris and Mickey Mantle of the New York Yankees were battling for the title of all-time home run king.

"If Mickey or Roger should hit two more homers at this point," the pitcher said, "each will have about a four percent increase. But with my two homers for the season, two more would represent a one hundred percent gain. That fact doesn't fool me into thinking that I will soon catch up to the big hitters or beguile me into a belief that my talents lie in hitting rather than pitching a baseball."

Things were not always so with West Germany and Japan. Nor will the conditions which brought about their rapid growth always obtain. Each nation's day comes, as Britain's did in the nineteenth century and that of the United States in the first three-quarters of the twentieth century.

Q. How do I determine which nations' days of prosperity and stock appreciation have arrived?

A. One way is by watching balance of trade data. This shows whether the country is selling more of its manufactured goods abroad than it buys in imported manufactured goods and/or raw materials. No nation can for long continue pouring out more wealth to buy than it receives from selling. Some felt that the United States could do this. The result was devaluation of the dollar and a further drying up of markets for American-made goods.

Another way to judge what's going on is by growth of gross national product (GNP). This is a yardstick for determining the overall output, etc., of a country. Unfortunately, each nation has a few gimmicks and wrinkles which it incorporates into calculation of GNP, so the data can't be compared country-to-country. But each country's GNP—provided it isn't tinkered with too much in order to produce favorable figures which will make the politicians in power continue to look good—can be compared to itself. That is, you can compare this year's GNP with last year's figures, note growth or regression, and compare that with the *rate* of growth and regression in other advanced lands.

Finally, study a nation's inflation rate. Given a high rate of inflation, trouble is bound to come. Eventually, manufactured goods will be priced out of world markets. Moreover, inflation distorts GNP and other study data so that they have little meaning.

Q. Why only advanced countries? Would there not be greater growth in a developing nation's stocks?

A. Keep in mind the analogy of the baseball hitters with two and fifty home runs respectively. Percentage gains, if made from low bases, are easy to achieve but don't really mean much.

Moreover, there exists in many of the developing countries a considerable hostility toward America and individual Americans. This spills over to color the attitudes taken against American investors, whose money the nations at first want to attract, but later want to seize when it appears that the ugly U.S. citizen whose funds built the plant is now taking his share of profits out of it. In other words, confiscations, seizures, currency blockages, and other things which can dwindle rather than increase your capital are more likely to occur in these developing lands than in nations of Western Europe and North America, or in advanced Japan.

Finally, with few exceptions, there do not exist ways in which an American or Canadian can conveniently purchase securities from developing nations. The trading machinery was designed to market stocks of advanced nations.

Q. How does one invest in these advanced countries?

A. If you want to do it the hard way, buy the stocks

themselves. Investors can do this either through brokerage houses which have operating offices in the countries
whose securities interest them, or by dealing directly
with a bank overseas. But that isn't the desirable way. It
involves red tape and tax complications in addition to
the immediate added cost of paying (if you're a U.S.
citizen or resident) the Interest Equalization Tax. That
tax is designed to overcome the inherent attraction of
some foreign stocks and bonds with yields which are in
most cases higher than the yields on comparable American investments.

The best way to handle things is by purchase of what
are called American Depositary Receipts. These evi-
dence the fact that there are on deposit certain shares
of the foreign stock in which an American investor is
interested. The "receipts"—generally called ADRs—are
issued against this stock. They trade freely. If you buy
from someone who is himself a U.S. citizen, or if the
ADRs are otherwise exempt from the Interest Equalization Tax, then no problems exist.

*Q. The problem is where to go to buy these ADRs
and from whom to purchase them. Give details, please.*

A. You can buy through most regular brokers whose
operations make it possible to purchase American and
Canadian securities. Simply say, "I want to buy Abracadabra, Ltd. ADRs."

You will find them quoted by bid and ask prices, just
as are other over-the-counter securities. In the course
of time, transfers are made, and your account with the
broker is debited (unless you operate on cash basis;
then he'll call on you for money in the routine way).
You have become owner of X shares of Abracadabra,
Ltd., fastest-growing widget maker west of the River
Rhine.

Q. Is there a mutual way of doing this, as with American stocks?

A. Definitely. If Japan is your growth place of choice, try Japan Fund, a closed-end fund (later, we'll examine what this means) listed on the New York Stock Exchange and purchasable there as you'd buy other American shares. There are similar closed-end funds which invest in other selected areas of the globe.

Points to Remember

1. There exists great growth potential in selected stocks of foreign companies.

2. But growth is neither automatic nor inherent. Study of a nation's prospects and of a company's posture are necessary before investment in overseas stocks. A complication to such study is the fact that national statistics are easier to find and to believe than some of the sparse, occasionally misleading, information put out in some nations. In such nations the stockholder, lacking a securities and exchange commission or other body whose aim is investor protection, finds himself regarded as an enemy from whom facts must be kept secret rather than as an owner entitled to be told how his company is faring.

3. Americans can buy securities of foreign companies (not all, however) as readily as they can purchase stateside stocks and bonds.

4. Along with greater growth in developing nations, there is greater danger to the investor.

5. American Depositary Receipts and overseas-slanted mutual funds are ways to invest easily in booming offshore economies.

Chapter Four

SOME LITTLE-KNOWN WAYS
TO BUILD CAPITAL

The dog nuzzling your hand while you read the afternoon paper might be the start of a program that brings in thousands of dollars toward a retirement estate, and continues to do so for years. The highball in your other hand is probably made of something that, used as investment and not merely for relaxation and pleasure, can produce sizable capital gains every year until the day you retire—even afterward. The comic book being read by your young son sprawled on the floor could bring in a profit as sizable as one-quarter million percent. The fish dish you had for dinner represents a tremendous industry; few retirement planners know that ordinary people who know no more about fishing than how to put a worm on the end of a line attached to a simple bamboo pole can reap enormous profits on the side while carrying on their regular businesses, jobs, or professional practices.

Q. Start with comic books. There's money in THAT?

A. Definitely. The following quotation is taken from a recent issue of my newsletter on business, investment, and consumer saving.

"At a recent convention of comic book collectors, otherwise mature men and women paid as much as $250 for items that had sold for only a dime in 1940. A quarter million percent increment, even spread over three decades, is good money.

"Investors have been attracted to the comic book field in hopes of being able to tell similar stories. But like gold rushes of the last century, the gold rush into the comic book trade has produced more anecdotes than actualities of fortunes. Not all 1940 comic books are worth a mint to the collector—in fact, most are relatively worthless. But if you're of a mind to try this off-beat form of investment, here are a few pointers:

"—First editions of comic books bring the most cash. The one that sold for $250 was MARVEL MYSTERY #1, containing the first appearances of several popular characters. A collector with no particular interest in a series may want to have the first issue of it just for the prestige of saying he owns it.

"—But beware. Others have used this trick. One collector saw an opportunity with publication of DARE-DEVIL #1. This was put out by Marvel Comics, publisher of MARVEL MYSTERY and several other sought-after comics. He bought one for his collection and six to sell. Then months later, he heard of a dealer who had 300 original copies. The market in old comics is large, but not sufficient to absorb 300 copies at premium prices.

"—The works of certain artists bring more money from collectors than first editions. In 1966, there was a surge of popularity for Frank Frazetta. Issues containing his artwork brought five times the price of comics from the same series done by other artists. But trends have to be watched closely; Frazetta's popularity is on the wane, and prices are being adjusted accordingly.

"—Current popular artists include Jack Kirby, Joe Kubert, Neal Adams, and Carl Barks. Coming into popularity are Mike Ploog, Barry Smith, and Berni Wrightson.

"—One pitfall is that bid and ask are often widely

separated. Dealers buy in quantity and must make valuable acquisitions pay for the lesser ones; these might sit on a shelf for years. Decide whether you'd rather have the quick return of selling through a dealer or the greater return of selling them yourself. A fine guide to pricing them has been published at $5.00 by Tom Overstreet, 2905 Vista Dr., Cleveland, Tenn.

"—Never buy from a dealer if your interest is investing. The dealer knows what it's worth, and he isn't giving bargains. Get your stock from the second-hand book stores.

"—Remember the Greater Fool Theory. Don't buy at a high price in hope that a greater fool will appear to take it off your hands at a higher. Investors have to know something of the values of comics to collectors."

Q. And the dog—how is he going to make money?

A. Peter is a fortyish father of five who lives in the suburbs on an acre of ground, makes adequate salary, and seeks a way to build up his estate at small cost with hopefully big results. Peter recently purchased a pedigreed dog for $100.

"Big thing," he told me, "is to be sure you have a breed that is in demand. That is more important than anything else if you are going to raise dogs for money and not merely for pleasure. There *is* a lot of pleasure in it, but that is not the object of breeding canines to breed a retirement estate."

Peter's first dog was a male. He found that after the dog had been trained for shows and had copped some impressive ribbons, owners of bitches of the same breed wanted his dog to father their animals' offspring. The deal was a cash fee plus the pick of the litter. Pete's cash went into a special account, which built up in geometric progression as the pick of the litter began to produce. Peter chose a bitch. She was trained, entered in shows, and soon bred to outside males to begin producing her own litters. Each litter meant $500 to $800 in sales as the pups became old enough to sell into good homes. Meanwhile, the original male continued to bring in fees—and additional salable pups.

Q. *What of the catfish?*

A. The following quote also comes from my newsletter:

"National consumption of fish is growing, and most of it is cat. A sizable portion comes from farms.

"Catfish growing is called farming because the fish are grown in the same way a farmer raises sugar cane or corn. He puts seeds into the ground and watches them grow. Then he harvests. A catfish farmer hires machinery to dig a big hole, 'plants' fingerlings, weeds out trash fish as the farmer removes trash plant growth, and eventually harvests his fish. It is usually done on a sideline basis. Sometimes friends get together to begin a fish farm. Many successful farms have been started by people who knew nothing about the industry to start.

"Catfish being raised on farms are a special new breed. A national market for them is growing rapidly. In 1968, according to the U.S. Dept. of Interior's Bureau of Commercial Fisheries, 80 million pounds of catfish were sold in the U.S. The Bureau estimates this figure will double by 1975.

"You can't get into operation on a shoestring, however. That is why several partners often join together. Some management time is needed along with money, and partners can split the working chores.

"Information is available from Catfish Farmers of America, Tower Bldg., Little Rock, Ark.; the Mississippi Research and Development Center, 787 Lakeland Drive, Jackson, Miss.; and Thibault Milling Co., P.O. Box 549, Little Rock, Ark. The U.S. Dept of Agriculture has a

study called 'Pond Construction and Economic Consid-
erations in Catfish Farming,' by Roy A. Grizzell, Jr., Soil
Conservation Service biologist.

"Catfish farmers are eager people. Their enthusiasm
should not let you fail to note that catfish farming can
have drawbacks and dangers as well as opportunities.

"—Says the U.S. Department of the Interior's Fish and
Wildlife Service in a booklet on farm reservoir fishes:
'This fish (channel cat) is in great demand as a food
fish. Unfortunately, the artificial propagation of the
species requires special techniques and farmers usually
must purchase fingerlings from commercial breeders. In
general, two or three growing seasons are required to
produce a marketable crop.'

"—If you own a catfish farm, you can't call a broker
and say, 'sell!' when you want out or require funds. If
you are in this with partners, then you will have even
more difficulty in selling a slice of a cat farm than you
would encounter as sole owner.

"—The investment is not small. However, it can be
financed as are other kinds of real estate.

"When all that has been noted, the fact remains that
catfish farming is a new, still uncrowded kind of side-
line that makes worthwhile money today."

*Q. How about the stuff in the highball glass? How
can that build my capital toward retirement?*

A. "Barring a return of prohibition, the growth of
scotch consumption will continue, and you can't lose
if you have money invested in maturing warehouse
whisky," the argument of scotch investment enthusiasts
goes. Of course this, like any other form of putting
money to work, can miss despite such enthusiasm. But
scotch investing is an interesting way that has made
many people rich. It is worth understanding.

Two kinds of whisky are manufactured in Scotland,

and only the *usquebagh* made in that land can legally
be called scotch. It has to be Scotch with a capital S
to be lower-case scotch whisky.

About two-thirds of your favorite scotch blend, assuming you drink as well as invest in the stuff, will be
grain whisky. This percentage varies from brand to
brand. The other portion will be malt whisky. Grain
provides the body, malt the flavor. Tastes in scotch
blending might change, and investors find the unchang-
ing grain often a stabler thing to own in hope of price
appreciation.

After the distiller has made whisky, it has to be aged.
Four years is now the legal minimum. Most is stored
for longer periods. The distiller might find himself with
great inventories of aging whisky but short of operating
cash because of the tie-up in the aging process. Enter
an investor, to whom the distiller sells ownership of the
stuff which is undergoing time's mellowing process in
bonny Scotland. That investor is you, if you decide
scotch is an opportunity as well as a beverage.

You buy in hope of capital growth. Consider some
figures on scotch consumption. In 1954, worldwide usage
was 17.6 million proof gallons. By 1957, thirst had increased to the point where 22 million proof gallons were
consumed. Voracious scotch drinkers used up 30.5 million proof gallons in 1960, 40.4 million in 1963, 50.6
million in 1966, and 62.0 in 1969. Consumption is expected by people who deal in scotch to be considerably
higher in years to come. "After all," one investor joked,
"we had a recession in 1970. That ought to make people
drink more than in happier economic times!"

According to figures released by Strathmore Distilling
Co., Ltd. of Glasgow, Scotland, "using median prices
per gallon, computed on a 16-year span, a $16,000 pur-
chase of new scotch grain whisky, sold when three years

old, would have returned $28,480—26 percent average profit per year."

In the past, success has not been inevitable or even. Strathmore's information sheet on a 1970 offering pointed this out:

"In order to ensure a fair portrayal, it should be stated that certain fluctuations occurred, evidenced by the following: 1958 distillation, $3.22 per gallon when new, achieved only $3.43 by 1962—although it is quoted today at approximately $12.00."

Serious losses were the lot of investors at one period. My earlier book *How You Can Beat Inflation* (McGraw-Hill) noted:

"During some of the years of the 1960's, when the glamor of being a whisky owner by the warehouseful had hit investors along with the idea that the use of scotch would never die, receipt prices suddenly took a plunge.

"The brisk market had encouraged some distillers to increase production in order to obtain whisky on which warehouse receipts could be sold to eager investors. Soon receipts glutted the market. Adding to the drop in price, some of them had been held with heavy loans on them, and when they declined hardheaded bankers sold the receipts to save their loans. That further depressed the market.

"The market came way back, and scotch receipts, handled with due caution and an awareness that nothing in this life is surefire, can serve as an effective inflation container."

You can deal with brokers here in the United States. There are two major firms whose ads are found regularly in financial journals. Or you can buy directly from an overseas distiller in the land of Robbie Burns. Their ads also appear in publications of finance.

Organized marketing machinery exists to dispose of your holding of highland broth when it comes to maturity. One distillery explains:

"All whisky eventually is sold to blenders for use. Although the main commerce is between distiller and blender, there has always been some portion held independently and such parcels might pass through many hands prior to the last sale. Whisky holders may sell to whomever they choose with no obligation to their original source of purchase.

"Traditionally, the largest independently owned parcels are often serviced by distilleries on a direct basis without fee as 'accommodation accounts.'

"Other independent transactions may be effected either on a person to person basis without assistance or through scores of Whisky Brokers located primarily in the United Kingdom. Such brokers are actively engaged in negotiating both purchases and sales, either from their own holdings or on a commission basis. Sales are simple procedures, consummated with no formal waiting period."

In addition to United Kingdom brokerages, those in the United States will attempt to market your investment but will not guarantee to be able to do so.

Sticky liquidity is a drawback. Disposal of warehouse scotch isn't like calling a member firm of the New York Stock Exchange to sell 100 shares of a stock if you should need money to finance Junior's emergency appendectomy.

You can't get income at first. But later, you might work a plan like this: Each year you purchase a batch of scotch. When the first purchase has matured, you can sell it, buy another equal to it which in its turn will mature in a few years, and pocket the difference. You have secured spendable income for the year. The next year another batch reaches selling age, and you do the same thing. You should thereafter always have an equal amount of warehoused scotch in your investment "port-folio" and each year be able to pocket as income the difference between cost and sales price (assuming, of course, that the stuff sells more with age added than when it was new).

To pyramid, you do as outlined above except that, instead of buying an equal amount of zero-age whisky to replace maturing scotch each year, you buy all that the proceeds will permit you to purchase. Gradually over the years (again, assuming ability to sell higher than you purchased), you should accumulate quite a position in potable, marketable spirits. Your capital, again making the gain assumption, will thus increase at (1) the rate of gain in value as maturity adds taste and usability to the whisky, and (2) the plowed-back rate of adding more and more whisky to your holding.

Recently, John B. R. Turner, Director of the Strathmore Distillery, wrote me: "A first venture should be considered not as a bold step for great profit, but as a latch key opening the door to discovery. . . . Can a minimum of $300 be too dear a risk?"

Points to Remember

1. Fortune-building techniques to triple your money and create a sizable estate with which to retire rich are not found only in the conventional areas of stocks, other securities, and real estate. Such offbeat ideas as canine raising, investment in scotch whisky, even comic-book collecting, offer sometimes fantastic profit.

2. With comic-book buying—where a dime book may increase in value to $250—it is wise to study trends of popularity and to know the artists and authors in current or coming collector favor.

3. Dog breeding can lead to pyramiding profits as the income from puppies and stud fees mounts up. It pays

particularly to concentrate on breeds enjoying maximum popularity among the public and fellow breeders.

4. Catfish farming requires more substantial capital but can be undertaken in partnership with friends or associates. It ties in with a tide of the times, running toward increased fish consumption and toward finding the fish on predictable farms rather than in the chancy streams and seas.

5. Scotch whisky tastes good if you like the stuff. It also offers opportunity for pyramiding profits if world consumption of highland dew continues to increase.

Chapter Five

THE FORTUNES IN GRAIN AND METAL

Not long ago, a voice spoke to the women of America. "You ladies are pretty good at buying eggs to make into omelets and to scramble, fry, or hard-boil. You know your beans about corn and wheat. You're pretty knowledgeable about purchasing bacon for your families.

"But we can't let you buy big lots of eggs on the commodities markets. You should not speculate in corn or wheat even if you do know all there is to know about cornflakes and bread. You're smart on bacon, but the pork bellies from which it is made should be forever forbidden to you."

So—in effect—spoke one of the largest brokerage firms in the world. With some exceptions it now forbids account executives to take commodity trading orders from the females of our species.

Was it right? *Should* women trade in eggs, pork bellies, silver, soybeans, wheat, wool, oats, orange juice, and others of the *contracts* traded on commodities exchanges? Should men? Should anyone? Should you?

An answer applicable to both men and women would be: not unless a great deal of homework and continuing study is put into it. Some sizable fortunes have been made in commodities. They have been made by hard-headed traders who took the trouble to learn the important things that affect success in one of the chanciest, most rewarding, and most dangerous investment fields of the world.

Foodstuffs and metals are very tangible. But commodities futures contracts are not. They consist of legal instruments which represent future delivery or purchase. You can, for example, contract via future purchase to deliver 18,000 dozen eggs in, say, June or December. You can also contract to sell those eggs. You can do likewise with 5,000 bushels of grain, 40,000 pounds of live beef cattle, 30,000 pounds of cocoa, 50,000 pounds of copper. If study of the facts about these and other situations convinces you that the price should go up before the contract comes due, you buy. If your homework tends to show a probability that the price will drop, you sell. If you are right you can gain a great deal, since margins in commodities are low, typically around 10 percent of the value. Thus a 10-percent increase in price would bring a 100-percent profit on money invested. Since a 10-percent move in the wrong direction could produce a 100-percent loss, you have to be mighty careful before making a decision.

That is why you should invest in commodities only after careful study.

Q. *How is such study carried out?*

A. One approach leads through the thing itself, whose markets, prospects and conditions a speculator studies closely to develop a working hypothesis for deciding whether it will (1) go up or (2) go down in price in succeeding months. However, this is only part of what our commodity trader-speculator-investor needs to know. He also needs to know *when*.

The commodity traders who ask *what* are termed fundamentalists. They look into the commodity itself to reach a conclusion as to whether probable future movement will be up or down. They must then assume that the conditions to bring about a new movement will eventually be recognized by the rest of the people who trade in the grain-metals-animals-eggs markets and that the buying or selling engendered by those who see things a little later than they became apparent will bring about profits. Speculator Sams seldom care whether the condition they foresee will result in a rise in price or a decline, for it is as easy to "go short" by selling commodities they do not yet possess as it is to "go long" by purchasing. Great wealth has been accumulated from time to time by forethought, if it is guided by the right facts and leads to correct conclusions.

However, sometimes speculators are right in their view but wrong about when the facts will come to majority attention with sufficient clarity to entice others into actions which fatten the speculator's account and up his tax bracket for the year.

When that happens, our trader is exposed to two dangers. The first and less worrisome is that capital might be tied up for weary months without producing anything except frustration. If capital is limited or too much of it goes too early into a situation like this, the ability to operate elsewhere might be badly curtailed. The next danger is worse. Occasionally a position in commodities can go wrong before it goes right and do this to such an extent that a margin call goes out. In general, no one is wise to let investments deteriorate that far, but it has happened before to Susie and Sam and may again.

Therefore smart commodity trader-speculators study two kinds of data, fundamental and technical.

Q. What does a fundamentalist ask before committing capital to commodity trading?

A. These are questions whose answer he requires:

1. *What will be probable production this year?*

Government agencies (the Department of Agriculture in the United States) report on crop production regularly. In addition, government experts make an effort to project probable production when the current crop comes to harvest in the case of certain commodities, or when cattle are led to slaughter, or when final mine production data are in. These projections are not 100-percent accurate, but they give a basis for figuring.

In addition, brokerage firms and other private sources make similar extrapolations.

2. *What are demand prospects?*

As the Little Red Hen said in the children's fable, "Who will eat my corn?" Probable demand for a product is as important as the expected-production information. Combined, the two data give an idea of whether prices could move lower or higher. Estimates are available from government and private sources, or you can make your own.

3. *Will competitive products come into the market?*

A few years ago the price of copper rose so high that electrical manufacturers began using aluminum for certain wiring, since prices of the latter industrial commodity had not risen. Some vegetable oils can be used interchangeably. The possibility of a competitive product's taking over if prices go high enough should be taken into account along with straight production-demand estimates.

4. *What is the news?*

I recall a cartoon of some years ago in which a man stood before a field of grain which was being rapidly devoured by locusts. He spoke on the phone to his broker: "I don't care what your research department says. Buy some corn and buy it fast!"

When new events come along, old estimates have to go out the window. This is especially true in a fast-moving field such as commodity trading.

Q. What is technical timing analysis?

A. Timing—the technical research we considered a few paragraphs back—is usually studied by means of charts. Chartists tend to make a mystique of their trade. It need not be mysterious at all. Most technical analysis is based upon support and resistance phenomena.

Chartists use a vertical line on ruled paper to show price action of a futures contract for one day. If the contract traded between a high of 2.40 and a low of 2.30 and the last trade was 2.35, the chartist would pencil a line from 2.30 to 2.40 and mark a horizontal dash at 2.35 to show the close. When prices keep bumping up to a level without being able to go through it, the level becomes a "resistance area." A breakout above, after repeated efforts have failed, indicates probability of heavy demand pushing prices still higher, chartists say.

When prices plot-plot against a bottom level without descending through it, the level is known as a "support line." A break below it has the same significance for probable descending prices as the breakout from a re-sistance level has for expected increased prices, chart students claim.

Charts of commodity futures can be kept by a trader, although few of them do this. It's easier to obtain them from commercial sources, and easiest of all to look at them in a broker's office without charge.

Q. How does commodity leverage work?

A. Over the course of a six-month period, a very swinging stock might double or, in a down market, be halved. An ordinary, pedestrian commodity might do the same in six weeks. A true swinger might do it in two weeks—even less.

Leverage is a big part of the answer. If a stock margined at 65 were to move up by 65/100, the holder would have doubled his invested capital. This would call for a $10 stock to move to $16.50, a $50 stock to $82.50, or a $100 stock to $165. Such moves do not come often or easily in stocks. But they do in commodities.

On soybeans or wheat the margin per contract might typically come to $600. If beans are at 2.20 and move to 2.32, there exists a 12-point profit on the contract and a consequent doubling of invested capital on the 5,000-bushel contract. A 65-percent move in a stock would call for a strong, long-term secular trend. A 12¢ move in beans could be mere fluctuation.

Points to Remember

1. Commodities such as vegetable oil, potatoes, silver, copper, pork bellies, plywood, and live cattle offer swinging ways to build up a capital stake quickly. However, a speculator who does things without proper study can lose his stake just as swiftly.

2. The answer lies in close and continuing study.

3. Two kinds of research are necessary. Fundamental study looks into the supply-demand relationships for the commodity and into general business conditions. Technical study goes into the matter of investor demand for *contracts* rather than industrial or other demand for the commodity itself.

4. Leverage in commodity contracts is greater than in ordinary investment media.

Chapter Six

CAPITAL GAINS FROM
RUN-DOWN HOUSES

Have you ever passed a run-down house in an otherwise "good" neighborhood and thought to yourself that it was a blight on a handsome street? Next time you see such a sight inquire whether the eyesore is for sale. It might represent capital opportunity for you. The remodel-and-resell market is one of the best ways to accumulate an estate toward retirement. It is also a fascinating sideline business.

It calls for: (1) moderate capital (the house can probably be bought with a nominal down payment, and repairs and remodeling can also be financed with small initial investment); (2) a piece of run-down property located in a neighborhood of more expensive homes which are well maintained; (3) a chance to buy the run-down property at distress price—for a real bargain is necessary if adequate profit is to be obtained from restoration; (4) an area which in fact as well as facade is of higher class than the run-down property.

People with large amounts of money develop whole subdivisions and suburbs. Using only moderate investment capital, you can develop single run-down homes, provided all four specifications above have been met. There are sizable percentage investment profits in it.

Q. Isn't the trend of population movement away from cities, and wouldn't this defeat the objective of finding run-down property in a neighborhood which won't also eventually run down?

A. "Eventually" is a long-term word. Anything might eventually happen. You want to avoid the neighborhood, street, or block which gives signs of deterioration in the next two or three years. Beyond that, you needn't worry. As a remodel-and-resell investor, you will have gone on to other (and possibly bigger) things.

Furthermore, all population trends are not away from the cities. My book *Nine Roads to Wealth* (McGraw-Hill) puts it this way:

"There is a new movement of people underway. If a time exposure picture were possible, you would see a broad flood moving out of the cities. You would also see a small stream moving back to the metropolis. Strange as it may seem, the backward river is the one which is increasing in volume. Sick of long travel via freeways to work inside the city, weary of the smaller selections found in suburban stores, frustrated by the tighter zoning which forbids a quick trip around the corner to a food or drug store, people who moved away from the city due to one set of aggravations are beginning to move back because of another set of annoyances."

Q. How does an investor not otherwise knowledgeable on real estate values determine whether a neighborhood is indeed sound?

A. You can learn a great deal from a quick ride through, provided you ask yourself the right questions about surrounding property:

- Are others in a state of disrepair? Peeling paint and sagging front steps are signs that others besides the owner of the property you're considering have allowed the neighborhood to become seedy. In such circumstances your potential buy, even at a bargain price, is probably no bargain.

• Are there children playing on neighborhood lawns? Families with young offspring tend to stay with a neighborhood and keep up its appearance. Older families, needing less room after the children move on, may be selling out, and the neighborhood is in more danger of sliding than if it has a population which will be around five to ten years.

• Is commercialism seeping in?

• Does the area have one- or two-family zoning? When multifamily zoning rules come in, property values of older sections often tail off.

• Is the asking price cheap in relation to surrounding property and in relation to what it will cost to do necessary repairs and remodeling?

• Will the house be marketable after I fix it up? If sales drag slowly in the area—you can learn something about this by talking to residents, by discussing the matter with a professional realtor, or by watching to see how long for-sale signs stay in front of other property—then it will probably pay you to avoid the property. Each month a house stays unsold after you've put it back on the market, your costs rise due to insurance payments, pro rata taxes, and the costs of upkeep such as having the grass cut and the sidewalks shoveled.

• Finally, find out whether property prices are on the upgrade. You can discover this by examining real estate transfers (usually public records) to see who bought where, from whom, and at what prices. Study property transfers in the area for several blocks to obtain a feel for whether neighborhood values are increasing or worsening.

Q. How much should I expect to make on a remodel-and-resell deal?

A. If you could expect profits rather than merely hope for them, real estate would be the only surefire business in the world. Obviously, it is not. You should *aim* to double your money. Here is some sample arithmetic:

- The price settled for the house is $20,000.
  You have to put down a payment of $2,000
- To put in needed changes will run another
  $5,000. You can borrow $8,000 from a local
  bank, making another down payment of $2,000
- You estimate insurance, taxes, and other
  overhead will be $1,000

Thus the total amount you will spend out of pocket, excluding amounts you borrow, is $5,000. You should aim for an $8,000 profit, pricing the house whose basic cost was $45,000 at $53,000. If you don't feel the neighborhood is good enough to make the house bring that after remodeling, then wash out the deal; it is not a sound one. Either your buying price is too high or the neighborhood is not as desirable as it seemed. A run-down house can be remodeled up to the level of its neighborhood, but not beyond it.

Q. What sort of repairs should I consider?

A. Only cosmetic ones which improve the looks at relatively small cost. Avoid structural work which adds to the lasting qualities of the house but, because it does not show, will probably add little to the eventual selling price when you put the house back on the market. Shoring a sunken house would be a structural change. Painting it or remodeling the bathroom would be cosmetic.

Certain changes nearly always make a house more desirable in a buyer's eye. One of these is kitchen modernization. Another is making over an old-fashioned bathroom. Adding a second bath to a one-bath house helps, and if you put it close to, above, or below existing plumbing lines, the cost need not be heavy. Addition of a carport helps.

Beware the building that has termite infestation. Getting rid of the insects won't be hard, but repairing the damage they have done might entail sizable structural work.

Points to Remember

1. In most "good" neighborhoods there are houses whose owners have permitted paint to peel, plaster to crack, weatherboards to crack off, lawns to overgrow with crabgrass. Such property represents a capital investment opportunity. The reason is that an owner—you in such a case—is able to upgrade a house to the level of the rest of the neighborhood. But he is not able, unless backed with nearly unlimited capital, to upgrade a whole neighborhood. And even well-heeled big investors attempting to upgrade neighborhoods sometimes find that the trends of tenant tastes are too strong to be changed.

2. However, even a run-down house in a promising neighborhood must be purchased at a bargain price in order to become profitable. Preferably, some real estate people say, you should seek to get it for the value of the lot alone. Such bargains can be had. It takes patience and a willingness to pass up house after house until the right chance is available.

3. Trends at present favor prudent investment in run-down houses because there is, in many areas, a move back to the cities by suburbanites who have found that the city disadvantages are equaled by fringe drawbacks such as crowded freeways, high taxes, smaller stores, and lack of public transportation.

4. A ride through the neighborhood should furnish answers to certain questions: Are surrounding homes

well kept? Are families with young children living in
the area? Is it becoming commercial? What are zoning
regulations? Will the house be marketable after repair?
The ultimate profitability of the remodel-repair venture
depends on the answers to those questions.

5. Advance arithmetic is essential. You should expect
to double the money you put into the venture in the
form of down payment, loan, taxes, insurance premiums,
etc.

6. If a house needs structural repair or structural remodeling, it is seldom a good buy for this kind of operation. Cosmetic repairs may pay off faster, cost less.

Chapter Seven

MAKING MONEY FROM LAND

The tight-money spasm of 1969 and 1970 played havoc with some real estate operations. It led pessimists to say: "Sure, fortunes were made from the land in the years that followed World War II. But that's all over." If you, too, believe it is all over, consider this statement made by former U.S. Secretary of the Interior Walter J. Hickel in a speech:

"About 70 percent of the people of the United States live on one percent of the land. Each year, three million more Americans are being shoehorned into cities that are already filled. It won't be long before eighty percent are living on one-and-a-half percent of the land."

And writing to his stockholders in a recent annual report, George H. Weyerhaeuser, chief executive officer of Weyerhaeuser Co., said: "Our nation is faced with a shrinking forest land base, a population explosion and urban sprawl. . . . There must be full public understanding that most material wealth comes from the land in one form or another."

On those statements rests the case for continuation of the trends that have made wise use and promotion of raw land a sound investment. The key word is *wise*.

Q. Why would land appreciation be "inevitable"?

A. Consider some of the factors behind the probable future growth of land values:

1. There is, as was noted in Chapter Six, a move back to the cities. Still, streams of people move out from the crowded concrete to find patches of green grass and houses not attached to each other like an endless string of frankfurters flowing off a meat-packing line. They are now moving from yesterday's suburbs, which are beginning to exhibit some symptoms of urban blight, to the exurbs, the "urbs" beyonds the suburbs. What was raw land yesterday is becoming valuable development property today. Tomorrow, it may be as paved-over and built-upon as the inner-city areas.

2. Wholly new cities are being developed where once swamps, deserts, or woods stood as nature made them thousands of years ago. Conservationists often deplore this change. It isn't my purpose to comment upon the desirability of thus changing wild lands to developed and inhabited areas; facts are facts alike to the conservationist and the urban builder, and this fact argues for further appreciation in raw land values. The new cities may be an important demographic fact of the seventies.

3. Different shopping patterns are developing. Once stores clustered together in downtown business districts. They were built up to the sidewalk and their walls touched one another; land was too valuable in the center of town for a single square inch to be wasted. Shoppers had to come to the store in public transit, walk about, then tote home their purchases on crowded buses or trains or else wait for overcrowded store delivery systems to get the purchases to their front doors.

Shopping habits began to change shortly after World War II when increasing prosperity made the prewar garage inadequate for a middle-class family's two vehicles. Now a shopper still goes to the store—but in her car, not on a bus, and only a relatively short distance to the outlying branch store rather than to the central commercial district. There she parks in a free, marked-off space and woe to any shopping-center developer who does not provide adequate parking. Shopping centers eat up vast amounts of land. The trend is not halting. It is accelerating.

4. Greater disposable income brings two-home living within reach of more people. "I want everything in our country weekend home that I have in our city house," one executive said in describing his second abode. "The idea of the second home is to relax—to have year-round vacations by getting away each Friday after work. No fun in owning such a place if it's the old, rude, crude sort of house beside a stream with which people were once satisfied. In my second home I want all the comforts of the first." Such second homes involve a prodigious need for raw law in the years ahead.

5. A final factor is the move of giant corporations into land development. Such companies as Westinghouse and Alcoa are no longer content with the electrical and aluminum fields. They are sizable factors in real estate as well. Their future moves virtually assure a liquid market tomorrow for property you buy for investment today—provided it is well and wisely bought.

Q. How does a relatively small operator—a man planning his retirement stake and not a giant operator with millions of dollars—benefit from this?

A. He needs to remember that appraisal of future opportunity, and efforts to bring it about, calls for understanding of two important words. They are: *value added*.

A veteran real estate operator with whom I discussed this says: "A parcel of dirt and scrub grass that has potential for becoming something better is the kind of deal out of which money is made. You have to depend upon the management of a corporation to add value to its stock. But *you* can add value to land."

Sometimes this addition of value happens because a retirement planner or other investor drains swamps, clears wooded areas, and constructs facilities which he can (hopefully) sell at a profit. But the addition is sometimes only that of an idea.

Q. For example?

A. "The next time you research land where, as one wit said, 'the hand of man has not trod,' don't merely look at its uneven places or its stony ridges," said my informant who invests in real estate. "Look at the possibilities for value addition. Are roads moving its way and will they make the land a quick drive from existing suburbs? A shopping center at such a place might be successful. Is the land near an airport? Perhaps a private long-term parking lot for travelers, with transportation to the ticket counters for parkers. Parking areas at some terminals are already overcrowded. Think of a medical complex, a resort development, a suburban office building, a marina, an industrial park, a condominium site.

"Ask yourself: 'Is something afoot or a new trend beginning that most people don't see as yet, but which will make those same people buy land here at higher prices tomorrow?'

"Often the idea of a value-addition is enough to sell land to a developer who will put up capital to make the value a reality. This calls for careful homework as well as vision. It can pay off handsomely."

One important trend from which tomorrow's raw-land investors might benefit is the move to condominium office buildings. Condominium apartments—in which each owner has title to his own living space with joint ownership and joint operational costs of halls, entrances, walkways, landscape, etc.—have been successful in the last decade. In the next ten years, the big deal might be in office buildings built and sold on the condominium plan.

(Something to keep in mind regarding condominiums is the fact that the Securities and Exchange Commission, which watchdogs American investors' interests, is tending toward rulings which establish condominium interests as securities within the meaning of the law which set the SEC to supervise securities trading. Best have an attorney knowledgeable about SEC matters at your side before undertaking anything in this area.)

Q. What buying tips are important in deciding on raw land as an investment likely to build a tripled retirement estate?

A. Whether value is added to raw land by building or by reselling with an idea as "fertilizer," it is important to remember the land investor's dictum that "well bought is half-sold." Land with potential, shrewdly judged in advance, will sell itself. Land without it cannot be peddled profitably on any terms. People who make their livings from raw land are insistent that the first question to ask yourself before buying is: "Who might repurchase this from me?" If no prospective class of purchaser is in view, then the land would be badly bought.

If a prospective user is in view, then the next question to ask before signing your name on purchase papers is: "How long will it take before the value-addition I have in mind can become reality, and before the kind of purchaser at whom I'm aiming can be brought to see this new factor?" A deal that will make 100-percent profit based upon capital tied up in down payment, monthly payout, taxes, and upkeep can be excellent if brought to fruition in a year, good if concluded in two years, worthwhile if done in three, and a dismal failure if pulled off only at the end of twenty years when the miniscule per-year gain might be wiped out by further inflation

Bargain land that can bring a big profit in a suitably short length of time is not to be discovered every day When it is found and when the arithmetic of probable land sale shows it to be a potential winner, then a wise real estate investor purchases all that he can finance and leverage with available capital. "No use trying to make a fortune on a lot or two," pointed out a developer of raw land. "You need acres to make a deal worthwhile Suitable land can't be found just by wanting to find it.'

Q. Comment, please, on raw-land financing.

A. Keep in mind that every lender is not set up to make every kind of loan. But he will try to bend your needs into his pattern. So it pays to have firm guidelines before you talk to a prospective lender. Know how much you want, how much interest you intend to pay (this must be realistic with going conditions), and how long you will want to take repaying the money. Then find a lender whose terms are suitable to you; don't settle for whatever the first fellow offers. You can haggle over rates; they aren't ironbound or unchangeable.

In this phase of high interest, try for a clause tying rates to a changing standard—for example, a set percentage over prime rate in New York—in order to avoid paying present high rates in a future time when interest may be lower.

Do business with a single source of funds once you find a suitable one. That way, your business is important to him and he'll try harder to help than he would for a casual drop-in borrower, even though that borrower might want to obtain sizable sums.

Generally, a bank or an insurance or mortgage company provides most of the sizable long-term needs of land investors. To finance part of a purchase price, the seller himself is frequently willing to take a note as partial payment in order to make the sale and for the advantage of spreading receipts over several years.

Before becoming beguiled by the appreciation possibilities and inviting financial leverage of land, an investor should be aware that a probability of further needs for land in the next decade does not guarantee that all land will appreciate in value. Some is likely to continue as desert, woods, or swamp. It's necessary to choose carefully, remembering that "well bought is half-sold" and that the key to profit is the concept of value added. And it is equally vital to be careful in buying land you cannot see, walk on, fly over, or appraise in the light of known conditions. Some "investors" in blue-sky property in distant states have found that their allegedly developed parcels of property were instead desolate desert, with Joshua trees the only vegetation.

Q. What are some of the dangers in raw-land speculation?

A. A big one is that you might be taken for a sucker. Only recently, Canadian operators painted beautiful pictures of land you could use for pleasure north of the border. The hunting—great. Fishing—nothin' like it. Close to interprovincial highways, and a stone's throw from an accessible airport. Run, man, buy!

And then repent. That's the way it went, for some of this land was under the Arctic Circle, some so far in the bush that Eskimos and Indians hadn't discovered it yet, part of it was under water. Worst of all, some was already owned so that any title you bought was worth a little less than the paper before it was printed on.

Reports have come about a renaissance in Southwestern desert-peddling. In one or two cases, the grand recreational property that sportsmen purchased proved to be on Indian reservations. And not long ago, charismatic Tennessee land peddlers sold—and transferred seeming title to—land on which the city hall of a sizable community stood.

The existence of a land law can't guarantee honest salesmanship any more than the existence of a law prohibiting murder means that killing has stopped. The law *can* help if you know what it does and if you take advantage of its provisions. Best of all, learn something about the firms from which you buy. Being far from home doesn't make an outfit automatically suspect, but it does mean you know less about it than you'd likely know about a local outfit. And get a property report.

Irked by shady practices of a small minority of land sellers, Congress in 1968 passed a law to protect the public. Under this law, you have a right to demand proof that the seller has a statement of record filed with the U.S. Department of Housing and Urban Development. Ask, too, for the property report, similar to prospectuses furnished to buyers of new securities. The law also provides that you must be told: the distances to nearby communities; whether there are liens on the property; whether contract payments will be placed in escrow; the availability of recreational facilities; the present and proposed utility services and charges; the number of homes currently occupied at the time you buy; whether there are soil or other foundation problems; and the type of title you will receive.

Points to Remember

1. Raw land has traditionally been the major road to riches for sizable American fortunes. It remains so today.

2. Over the history of North America, land has steadily, if irregularly, increased in value. Certain trends currently in force almost guarantee that raw land (although not

necessarily every parcel of land) will continue to appreciate.

3. Addition of value—building, concept, sales pattern —is the secret of making raw land bought today worth more tomorrow and of avoiding the slow and uncertain-as-to-time effects of inflation and raw-land needs.

4. Observance of certain buying methods can help. As the old real estate adage runs, "Land well bought is half-sold."

5. Since much depends upon leverage, knowledge of financing methods and trends is of prime importance.

6. And so is awareness of the dangers that lurk when you buy land far from home, sight unseen.

Chapter Eight

REAL ESTATE INVESTING
THE "REIT" WAY

"A fellow who doesn't know much about Wall Street and has no time for intensive reading can be successful buying mutual funds which furnish professional management and diversification," a teacher planning for retirement told me. "Why hasn't somebody done the same thing for real estate?"

Someone has. They call it the real estate investment trust—REIT for short. REITs are diverse as well as diversified, so it is well to know the kinds before you rush out to buy shares in one of the many trusts that are available today.

Q. What precisely is a REIT?

A. In *New England Economic Review*, Peter A. Schulkin of the Federal Reserve Bank of Boston laid down five signposts of a real estate investment trust:

"1. The REIT must be a passive investor rather than an active participant in the operation of its properties. But the active manager of a REIT's properties can own up to 35 percent of the REIT's stock.

"2. At the end of each quarter 75 percent of the value of the REIT'S total assets must consist of real estate (including mortgages), cash, cash items, and government securities.

"3. At least 100 persons must own shares, and five or fewer persons cannot own more than 50 percent of the shares during the last half of any tax year.

"4. At least 75 percent of the gross income of the REIT must be derived from rents, mortgage interest, and gains from the sale of real estate.

"5. At least 90 percent of the REIT's ordinary income must be distributed to the shareholders within one year after the close of the taxable year."

According to *Financial Analysts' Journal*, real estate investment trusts had $4 billion in assets in 1970. This is small by comparison with mutual funds' $50 billion, but it is expanding while the amount of money invested in mutual funds has not appreciated in several years.

Q. Are REITs pretty much alike?

A. No more than mutual funds. An investor should understand the groupings:

• Construction- and development-loan REITs. Their investments are restricted. Construction loans are secured by first mortgage and generally used to finance building of single homes, apartments, and even commercial structures. Development loans go to site improvement, land clearing, and leveling. C & D loans have attractive yields. They run as high as 14 percent and enable a REIT to pay out handsome amounts.

• Long-term-loan REITs, some of which specialize in equity ownership. That is, they own, and do not merely lend money on, apartment buildings and other sizable structures.

• Mixed REITs put some of their money into C & D loans, some into long-term loans, some into equity ownership.

Sometimes the loan portfolio contains a high proportion of government-guaranteed loans. These have less risk but don't pay as much. Be aware of the difference. You can tailor the risk you want to accept by examining the portfolio of a REIT.

Q. Will they redeem shares as mutual funds do?

A. Most mutual funds are *open-end*. That is, they will sell shares to you based upon net asset value (the total value of stocks they hold, less debt if any, divided by number of shares). And they will redeem based on the net asset value if you want to sell.

Real estate investment trusts generally follow the closed-end setup of the minority of mutuals. They have a set number of shares and that's it. The shares are traded on an exchange or over the counter as are shares of other corporations. Investors buy and sell from and to each other rather than dealing with the issuing company. This setup is necessary because while mutuals can value stocks twice a day, REITs can't compute the values of loans and land with equal readiness.

Q. Therefore REITs are bought for income and not capital gains?

A. To quote from the Federal Reserve study:

"Although virtually all the earnings of long-term mortgage and C & D REIT's are paid out in dividends, the prices of the shares of these REIT's can and in some instances have, appreciated substantially. Price appreciation can result from three factors. First, the legally required dividend payout may be high enough to cause the price of a REIT's shares to increase. Second, if a REIT can profitably leverage, i.e., exploit the difference between its lending and borrowing rates, a REIT can increase its earnings (and dividends) per share and cause its share price to rise. Third, if a REIT is able to sell new shares at a price such that the dividend yield on its shares is lower than the yield it can obtain on invested funds, it can increase its earnings per share and share price, i.e., the REIT can 'leverage' by exploiting the difference between its cost of equity capital and the rate it obtains on invested funds."

Q. Will I get professional management as in a mutual fund?

A. Yes. And as in a mutual fund, the professional management may be smart or inept. When choosing a fund, investigate management's possible interest in side-line income for itself.

Example: You may find that the REIT you're checking on compensates management with an advisory fee. In addition, management may use the REIT to generate business for its allied building and other real estate activities.

Q. What pitfalls exist?

A. Fluctuating levels of interest rates are a factor. A REIT has to balance incoming capital cost with the relatively fixed (because long-term) interest rates it receives.

Moreover, the field could become overcrowded so that competition for loans would reduce profitability.

And as always with an organization that lends money, there are repayment risks. Although group experience to date has been favorable, different economic conditions might bring a change.

Points to Remember

1. The mutual fund concept in stocks calls for many investors pooling capital to spread risk and enjoy diversification and professional management benefits none could achieve alone. (Mutual funds are discussed in detail in Chapter Eleven.) This concept of investing has

been extended into real estate through the real estate investment trust, or REIT.

2. REITs held assets of $4 billion in 1970. This amount is small compared to the vast holdings of mutual funds, but it is growing.

3. REIT setups differ widely. Some make construction and development loans. Others go in for longer-term loans secured by motgages. A third group makes both kinds of investment. And a fourth kind of REIT goes in for equity ownership of real estate.

4. Unlike mutual funds, REITs, by their nature, cannot redeem shares investors want to cash. However, most stocks are sold on exchanges.

5. REITs are vulnerable to fluctuating rates of interest and to the effects of competition.

Chapter Nine
BONDS FOR BIG MONEY GAINS

All through those troubled, tight-money times in the latter years of the sixties, retirees were told, "Put your money into bonds. You won't ever see any capital gains, but you'll get a lot of interest." It was a negative sort of recommendation. For those not yet arrived at retirement, such a prospect was hardly inviting.

Then suddenly in the latter months of 1970, as business conditions deteriorated rapidly into recession, the monetary fathers of the country began to swell the money supply. Interest rates dropped slightly, then dropped more—and finally tumbled.

Bond prices took off like a rocket. "Don't tell me about stock prospects," one observer noted. "The money is being made in bonds." Bonds are like that. They sit as unwanted as an orphan with measles until suddenly the blotches go away. Then investors see a pretty girl instead of a waif. What remained following the sudden takeoff of bond prices and prospects in late 1970 and early 1971 was an investment medium that, many people discovered, was very little understood.

Bonds deserve some understanding.

Q. How are bonds different from stocks?

A. Stockholders own a corporation. Bondholders are the people who lend money to it. A bond is an IOU issued by the federal government, by a state or local government, or by a company. People who buy bonds lend their money. The bond stipulates when the principal is to be repaid and what interest rates will be given to bondholders.

Unlike the IOU you might have from an individual, bonds are negotiable; that is, they can be bought and sold. It is the owner of the moment to whom the issuer owes money at maturity and to whom he pays interest meanwhile.

Dividends on stocks can go up if the company prospers, down if it has a bad year. The interest on bonds does not change. If the bond issuer is in financial trouble, he sometimes suspends interest payment altogether; however, this almost never happens in the case of quality, high-rated bonds.

Q. What types of bonds are available?

A. One way to classify bonds is according to the issuer. As mentioned, bond issuers include the federal, state, and local governments and companies. The highest rates of all are paid for the obligations incurred by the U.S. government. U.S. Treasury debt instruments are known generically as *Treasuries.* Those maturing in one year or less are called *bills;* obligations from one to seven years are termed *notes;* with a still longer maturity period (from issuance date), they are called *bonds.* The terminology change is for Treasuries only and has no real effect or importance from the investor's viewpoint.

Some kinds of government bonds are not direct Treasury obligations, but their interest payment and principal safety are considered as sacrosanct as Treasuries'. These are the IOUs of semigovernmental bodies such as the Federal National Mortgage Association or Federal Home Loan Bank.

States, cities, counties, school boards, etc., also issue bonds of varying maturities. These are known collectively as *municipals*. Under most conditions, their interest is tax-exempt. Advantages, pitfalls, and uses of municipals will be considered in greater detail in Chapter Ten.

Companies also issue bonds. Some are as strong and prestigious as American Telephone or General Motors Acceptance Corp. Others are as shaky and speculative as bonds of Joe's Widget Works. Bond ratings help you determine the extent of risk among these corporates.

Q. Is that all the story on bonds?—governments, municipals, and corporates?

A. Not entirely. Some bonds are *mortgage bonds*, secured by a mortgage on the issuer's property. Theoretically, bondholders can have this property sold at the courthouse door if they are not paid. In practice, the protection is not as valuable as it seems: Often, if real trouble arises, so many other debts exist that a company is thrown into bankruptcy—and the bondholders must stand in line along with those who sold the equipment, made straight loans, or have routine bills run up by the unhappy issuer. Similarly, in the municipal field, some bonds are "full faith and credit" obligations, backed by everything the issuing unit possesses.

Among the corporate bonds, some have certain kinds of income set aside for their interest payments and principal retirement. In the municipal field, bonds occasionally are secured by particular taxes.

Other corporate bonds are called *debentures*. These are unsecured. It might appear on the surface that a mortgage or even a dedicated-income bond would be inherently safer than a debenture. But this is not always so. Even an unsecured obligation of a prime issuer is safer than a mortgage bond of a shaky outfit.

Q. What is a high rating? How can I avoid bonds of low rating and questionable safety?

A. Bonds are rated by boards of experts from Standard and Poor's Corp. and from Moody's Investors Service. The ratings range from AAA downward, with higher ratings indicating lessened risk in the opinions of the rating organizations. Ask your advisor or broker for lists of high-rating bonds.

Q. Do bond prices always go up when interest rates drop, and down when interest rates increase?

A. Consider a bond issued at 5 percent in a time when that was the going interest on high-grade debts. When interest rates rose so that debits of similar quality were paying 8 percent, the bond had to drop to about 62½ ($625 for a $1,000 bond) in order to pay such an interest on market price. If you bought at par of $1,000, you lost capital value. Then if the prevailing interest rate went back to 5 percent, the bond would bounce back to $1,000. Those investors who purchased at 62½ had a sizable capital gain.

Q. I've heard it said that bondholders are born losers because bonds have been poor long-term investments in the last twenty years. Please comment.

A. "Loser" and "winner" are not absolute terms. The investor interested in high yield has not lost on the big-pay 8- and 9-percent bonds he bought in the bear market years of 1969 and 1970. But the investor who purchased at times of lower prevailing interest certainly did lose. So the bondholder's losing or winning depends in part upon when he purchased bonds. When the bond market bottomed out in late 1970 and the interest rates dropped so dramatically, bond prices soared. The bondholders who purchased during the big-yield days won in two ways: They retained the big interest returns for which they bought (these, as noted, continue to be paid until bonds mature)—and they watched the value of their in vestments rise because bond prices increased due to the lowering of yields.

Q. How are capital gains secured in bonds?

A. By purchasing bonds at times of high interest rates when the prices of older issues are depressed (recall that 5-percent bond used earlier as an example) and then leveraging them as much as possible.

Assume that you purchased the 5-percenter at $625 for a $1,000 bond and that improving interest conditions drove rates down so that the bond bounced back to $1,000 "par." You would have a very hefty capital gain. If you leveraged the purchase, the gain could be tremendous.

Frequently, banks will lend about 80 percent of market value on good quality bonds. So you could put up 20 percent, or around $125 per bond to buy a package. On an investment of $125 per bond, which then appreciated $375 per bond, the gain would be about 300 percent! Such growth is not achieved in many fields.

Q. Where can I obtain interest rate information?

A. Write to the Board of Governors of the Federal Reserve System, Washington, D.C., asking to receive regular weekly mailings of interest rates. Write also to the Federal Reserve Bank of Saint Louis for their regular monetary mailings.

Points to Remember

1. A generation of investors was trained to regard bonds as stodgy investments suitable only for those in need of dependable income. They are, in fact (and at certain times), vehicles for sudden and sizable capital growth.

2. Bonds are not alike. There are different kinds of

bonds and different kinds of issuers. Rating agencies help you to choose by putting alphabetical tags on them denoting comparative quality.

3. Bond prices go down when interest rates are high, and bounce back up when the interest rate cycle swings downward. Therein lies a retirement-estate builder's opportunity to make his capital increase.

Chapter Ten

HOW TO AVOID TAX ON
INVESTMENT INCOME

An income without taxes seems utopian, or a Communist promise—certainly unrealizable. Yet it can be achieved by you, me, or any retirement planner who knows the ways in which some investments create income free of the bite of the federal (and in some cases, state) tax collector.

Q. For example?

A. The most obvious way to render income exempt from taxation is by purchasing municipal bonds. But this is not wise for every retiree or prospective retiree— municipal-bond salesmen won't always tell you that— nor is it the only way to shelter your income where the tax collector can't get at it.

Q. Let's start with municipals. What are they?

A. They are the IOUs of governmental bodies below the federal level—states, cities, counties, school boards, taxing districts, bridge and toll road authorities and the like. By law, the income you receive as interest from these bonds is not subject to federal taxation. In many cases, it is exempt from state income taxes as well in the state where the bonds were issued.

Obvious questions arise: If this is so good, why doesn't everybody own municipals? Why should anyone buy ordinary corporates and other debt instruments discussed in Chapter Nine? There is a good reason: municipals do not pay interest rates as high as other bonds of equal rating. Their attraction is chiefly for those in higher brackets during the years when they are building toward retirement, or those who invest enough money in bonds to make the saving sizable.

For example: A municipal pays 4 percent, a good corporate bond 5½ percent. If you are in a 20-percent tax bracket, the municipal is paying 4-percent real income, the corporate bond 4.4-percent after taxes. But if your bracket is 50 percent, your saving on the tax-free feature is large enough to make the municipal very attractive.

There's an angle to all of this. That is plow-back. Suppose you put back all income into added investment during the years that precede retirement. Then you are obviously able to parlay more dollars in a municipal, where everything received is available for reinvestment, than in a security, part of whose income must be saved out for payment of year-end taxes. The compounding effect can become considerable over the years.

Q. Are municipals sound or risky investments?

A. They are like stocks, other bonds, real estate, and most other things in this fluctuating world. Some municipals are of higher quality than others. Ten years ago I would have been able to state that all municipals were of at least relatively high grade. This is no longer true. Groaning under higher taxes than ever before, burdened by demands for welfare, highways, added police, and other necessary services, state and local governing bodies find themselves increasingly strapped. Professional investment services have lowered the ratings of many places—New York City is an outstanding example. So you'd better look carefully at what you buy since safety of principal is a prime consideration in retirement planning.

Q. Sometimes bonds are quoted at "yield to maturity," which is different from the actual interest percentage. Please explain.

A. If you buy a bond for $600 and it pays you $30 per year, you have a straight yield of 5 percent (arrive at yield percentage through dividing interest by cost). The bond will mature, say, in 1980 and will be paid off at par of $1,000 at that time. So there is a $400 gain in there as well as the immediate interest payments. In calculating yield to maturity, statisticians count in annual increments of this kind as well as the interest.

Q. What effect will inflation have?

A. Probably a great deal. You should count upon at least a possibility (I believe a probability) of inflation continuing and perhaps getting worse. Consider whether, in your own individual circumstances and given your particular retirement plans, the tax-exempt feature of municipal bonds is enough to compensate for potential loss of purchasing power. There isn't a "right" answer to this. You have to determine whether you want to bet on inflation stopping or going on, decreasing or increasing. None of us possesses a workable crystal ball. But figure that if inflation continues, it will affect all investments of fixed dollar income such as municipal bonds.

Q. Would municipals work well in a Keogh retirement plan for self-employed people?

A. The tax-exempt status of current income generated by the bonds' interest would not be as important. While the preretirement period exists and the accumulative phase of a Keogh package is in effect, income from investments is sheltered. You don't need two tax exemptions at this time (later on, things are different).

Q. What other tax shelters exist in addition to municipals?

A. One can be found in the dividends of certain public utility companies. On occasion, different accounting methods are required for regulatory and taxation purposes. This can lead to a situation in which part or all of a utility's dividends are considered return of capital rather than income. Ask your broker or investment counselor for a listing of utilities whose dividends have this feature.

Q. What about the taxes on stock rather than cash dividends?

A. Tax laws change and the status of each taxpayer differs. You will do well, therefore, to consult a tax adviser on applicability to your own case. But in general, it is possible to sell a stock dividend when received and, if the base stock on which the dividend was paid had been held the minimum period to qualify for long- rather than short-term treatment should it (the base stock, not the dividend) be sold, then the dividend can be a long-term capital gain when converted into cash. You don't escape taxation that way, but you move things into a lower bracket.

Points to Remember

1. Income from the bonds of counties, states, cities and towns, taxing districts, etc., is usually free from federal income tax and often exempt from state income tax in the state of issuance.

2. This permits a retirement-estate builder who is in

a higher tax bracket (which is important because yield is generally lower on these municipals and becomes advantageous only to those whose taxes are in a major bracket) to plow back the income into more investments without suffering a tax penalty.

3. Municipals are of generally high quality, but with each bond this needs to be investigated because some issuers' ratings have deteriorated in recent years. An example is New York City.

4. Some of the dividends of some public utilities are likewise tax-exempt and so permit plowing back income into extra capital without losing any to the tax collector.

5. Under many circumstances, receipt of stock dividends does not entail tax penalty until sold, and then as capital gains (depending upon length of holding of base stock).

Chapter Eleven

THE MONEY IN MUTUAL FUNDS

More than 50,000 common stocks are publicly traded.
How does an investor intent upon making his money
stretch into affluent retirement choose among them? The
problem is not simple. Before me is a compilation of
results from theoretical investment of $10,000 in each
of the big blue-chip stocks that make up the Dow Jones
Industrial Average. The table assumes investment of
$10,000 on January 1, 1934, and sale on December 31,
1969, thirty-five years later. Variance in results is as-
tounding:

If you had put the theoretical $10,000 into Eastman
Kodak (the best performer) in 1934, you would have
had $659,617 in 1969. But if your choice had been Allied
Chemical, your $10,000 would have grown to only
$15,096 in 1969—not sufficient to keep you abreast of
the inflation since World War II.

Because no one possessed a crystal ball in 1934, or
has such a handy tool for choosing investments today,
people who put aside money toward their support in
retirement have a problem distinguishing future East-
man Kodaks from the plodding Allied Chemicals.

The answer is found in one statistic: The median return from investment in the thirty stocks that make up
the DJIA was more than satisfactory; the venerable
Dow appreciated approximately 650 percent in thirty-
five years. This was not as good as its best performer,

but quite sufficient to make an investor's capital grow satisfactorily. Of course, you can't buy a stock called Dow Jones Industrial Average. You can, however, buy mutual funds to give this kind of median performance.

A mutual fund, by definition, pools the capital of many investors. By having—as a group—a great deal of money to invest, it can put the money into many stocks, achieve diversification, and enjoy results of the type achieved by the Dow Jones Industrial Average—and hopefully better.

Q. Didn't some of the "performance" and "go-go" mutual funds show pretty bad losses in recent down markets?

A. "Pretty bad" is an understatement. Some of them flopped almost totally. It became apparent after the fact that they had often relied upon phony valuations of restricted securities and upon other accounting shenanigans to make competitive showings. The Securities and Exchange Commission has since issued rulings which make this sort of practice illegal.

Still, the best performers of one year are the poorer performers of later years, and it pays to keep a careful eye on what you're doing.

Q. How does a retirement planner distinguish between latter-day go-go performers and the more solid, stable funds?

A. It's assumed that he is wise enough to look over a fund's prospectus before buying its shares. He should examine the makeup of its portfolio. Are the corporate names those everyone knows? Or are they the far-out stocks that fared so well in 1967 and 1968 but fell so badly in 1969 and 1970? If the latter, the mutual is probably a "gunslinger" rather than a conservative growth fund.

Q. Some funds don't pay out as much income as I can get now from bonds. So why buy the fund?

A. There are many good reasons for investing in bonds under present conditions (Chapter Nine discussed them). But as a prospective, rather than an arrived, retiree you are looking for some capital enhancement instead of high current income, which you'll need after actual retirement.

Hopefully, a sound mutual fund should be at least partly in equities with growth potential. Its portfolio components should also have possibilities of paying higher dividends as you go along (bond yields are fixed and won't change) so that by retirement time you might be receiving a larger yield than if you had gone in for a return that is high now but lacks enhancement possibilities.

Q. Please comment upon compounding of income from a mutual fund.

A. In the years preceding retirement, many people don't need immediate income and so follow a policy of buying more shares with the dividends they receive. Most mutual funds will plow back the payout for you on an automatic basis if you ask them to do so. That's compounding. Next year, the additional shares bought with plowed-back income of this year will produce still higher yield, to plow back for yet more yield the following year. Such plow-back is a sound policy during pre-retirement years, provided the income isn't needed for current living costs.

Q. What about dollar-cost averaging? What is this, and do you recommend it?

A. A cynic once defined dollar-cost averaging as the throwing of good money after bad. It works this way:

You put in a steady, unvarying amount each period (monthly, quarterly, semiannually, etc.). This lets you buy more shares when prices are down, fewer when they are up. And, if all works as the statisticians assume it will, your average cost over a long period should be less than market value.

But there are gimmicks in this statistical paradise. Such averaging works *if* things go ever upward; and *if* you pick a stock that enjoys uninterrupted years of appreciation in earnings and price; and *if* you have unlimited capital and courage to continue socking money into a declining stock, and *if* prices always go up after they go down.

Unfortunately, prices of stocks do not invariably come back. American Tel was 75 in 1965; it is 45 as this is written. U.S. Steel was 109 in far-back 1959; currently it is around 30. The giant duPont sold at 261 in 1965 and under 120 in 1970. Stocks of lesser quality have sometimes fared worse.

In mutual funds the presumption is that management will switch out of downgrading stocks and into better issues. In practice, most of the time it does, but it sometimes fails.

Better, in my opinion, not to dollar-cost average either in mutual funds or individual stocks.

Q. Are all mutual funds alike?

A. By no means. I divide them into the following major groupings: growth funds, slow-growth common stock income funds, "balanced" income funds, special bond funds, geographical funds, funds devoted to certain industries, new directions funds, special method-of-investing funds, and funds that buy other funds instead of stocks and dual funds.

Q. Please explain "load" and "no-load."

A. "Load" is a selling commission. It is added on to the net asset value per share. Selling loads might run as high as 8¾ percent. "No-load" funds are sold without this commission. You usually have to buy them directly from the fund itself since investment dealers prefer not to offer no-loads. Existence or absence of a load should not be your only criterion in choosing a fund.

Q. I want moderate-to-fast capital growth. How can I judge the ability of a mutual fund to produce this for me?

A. There are a number of statistical services which compute a fund's current growth for you. This does not guarantee that such growth will carry into the future, of course, or even that there will be growth at all. But it is all you have to go on, and in general the best way (I believe) to judge human abilities is by what the humans in question have been able to do in the past.

My own weekly publication, *The Markstein Letter*, offers a model portfolio composed of funds which I feel at any given moment qualify for expectation of fast growth. (The *Letter* also recommends common stocks to which growth criteria apply.)

Points to Remember

1. Mutual funds offer investors participation in a package of securities professionally chosen for specific objectives.
2. Some funds seek appreciation, others stability, still others high current income, and some a combination of two or all of these. It is important to know a mutual fund's objectives before buying its shares, and to be certain these objectives are the same as those an investor seeks.
3. Some funds flopped badly during bear markets. In-

vestors must beware of any fund if its performance turns
down.

4. Study a fund's prospectus; know not only what aims
it professes to accomplish, but the portfolio components
by which it expects to turn these aims into realities.

5. Statistical gimmicks such as dollar-cost averaging
should be avoided in mutual fund investing—and in
any other kind of retirement-estate planning.

Chapter Twelve

HOW STOCK MARKET CHANGES CAN MAKE YOU RICH

There was a time when you could easily tell the speculator in stocks from the conservative investor seeking to build an estate for retirement. The speculator bought and sold stocks, moving quickly from one to another. The solid investor bought and held stocks, never—or practically never—selling them.

According to financial folklore, the investor tended to pile up a long-term estate while the swift-moving speculator might—and often did—move swiftly into the poorhouse. However, many persons seeking to build estates through staid long-term, never-sell investment found in 1969 and 1970 that they were rapidly growing poorer as stock prices tumbled, while some of the smart speculative operators sat on the sidelines with a profit as the stock market turned long-termers into nervous wrecks.

The fact is, a time inevitably comes when you should sell all stocks. If you can recognize this time—no impossible task—you will conserve capital built up over the years *and be able to buy more shares when a bear (down) market eventually turns to the bullish (up) side.*

Q. What are some of the ways an average investor can tell when the stock market is about to slide as it did in 1969 and 1970?

A. Start by watching the outward signs. You can get a feel for the market's degenerating health from these telltale signals:

• "Value" becomes a valueless word. No one cares about corporate soundness, balance-sheet data, or even earnings trends. Investors want action.

• Interest is high in cat-and-dog stocks. Wall Street applies this uncomplimentary term to low-priced stocks in which speculative interest grows toward the feverish end of a long-drawn-out bull market.

• Optimism is rampant. Everybody knows that bad times won't ever come again, and a pessimist is hard to find in brokerage boardrooms.

• Stock price declines outnumber advances, even though market price averages are going up. The total of advancing and declining stocks can be found on financial pages. When downs outnumber ups consistently for a lengthy period even though prices of market averages increase, the market is probably in danger because the average goes up only by action of a decreasing number of stocks.

• There is wide public participation. Everyone you meet, from elevator operator to shoeshine boy, is in the market.

When you see those signs, the market is in a top area. It may not tumble immediately, but great danger is present.

Q. For example?

A. Let's take the 1969–70 stock slide. The market decline started at a high around 985, as measured by the familiar Dow Jones Industrial Average. Say, for the sake of easy figuring, that you had $985 invested. By May 1970 your theoretical investment in the Dow average was down in value to $630. You would have lost 36 percent of your retirement stake.

Now assume that you were too smart to let this happen. You sold at $985. At $630 you decided to buy back. Instead of 1 "share" of this average of the market, your $985 would now buy approximately 1½ shares. Even at the low point, you would have lost nothing—unlike the sad investor who held on. And you would be in a better position to participate in any coming rise because you would possess 50 percent more shares. A rise back to $985 would break him even. It would show you a sizable profit ($1,402 versus $985).

Q. Some of the telltale signs are nebulous. Is there anything more definite I can watch?

A. Try the monetary statistics of the Federal Reserve. One of its series has an interesting ten-year history of correctly correlating with every upturn and downturn in stock prices.

Monetary theory is the "in" thing in economics. Its gurus are Dr. Milton Friedman of the University of Chicago and Darryl Francis, President of the Federal Reserve Bank of Saint Louis. Simply stated, their economic school holds that all booms are fueled by an increase in money. A decrease—even a leveling-off—in money tends to bring on recession. Even the expectation of a recession generally means lower stock prices.

The indicator of money activity which appears most tuned to stock price movements is called "Reserves of Member Banks." You can obtain this and other data series by asking the Federal Reserve Bank of Saint Louis to send them to you; there is no charge.

Most smallish stock market trends have little significance. But if a stock trend change is confirmed by a similar upward or downward change of direction in the "Reserves of Member Banks" series, there is strong probability that the new move by the stock market will be an important one. In watching either stock market or money reserves trends, you must ignore little wiggles; concentrate upon what appear to be longer-term direction changes.

Q. Someone said that the market is only a mirror of the economy. What other watch can be kept upon underlying economic conditions?

A. The National Bureau of Economic Research has divided economic data into three groups: leading, coincident, and lagging indicators.

Leading indicators tend to turn consistently upward or downward before similar turns in the general level of economic activity. In addition to the empirical fact that the leading indicators behave this way, there is sound rationale behind NBERs conclusion: incoming factory orders, construction awards, etc., necessarily precede the actual manufacture and sale of goods or the erection of a building. Therefore, leading indicators tell an observer where the economy is going to be several months hence.

Coincident indicators move together with the economy, gross national product, factory sales, etc.—with things going on at the moment.

Lagging indicators are those whose turns upward or downward generally happen after the recession or the new boom has started; a rise or fall in the unemployment rate, for example. Their value is confirmatory.

You can observe action of the leading, coincident, and lagging indicators by subscribing to *Business Conditions Digest,* a U.S. government publication available from the Superintendent of Documents, Washington, D.C. 20402, at $16 per year.

Q. I have heard it said that bull and bear market swings come faster these days than they once did. Is that so? If so, does it affect what has been discussed above?

A. Yes, they come more quickly. And yes, they still have validity—much more so since the dangers and opportunities are multiplied in frequency and number.

The way things used to be, a bull market generally lasted three or four years, a bear market a year or so. Now the swings are getting shorter, and a bear swing's length approaches that of a bull market. Confirming this observation is a tabulation in which the following signals were made.

> October, 1966, buy
> December, 1968, sell
> May, 1970, buy
> April, 1971, sell
> November, 1971, buy
> April, 1972, sell
> July, 1972, buy

Thus the first bull movement was twenty-six months in duration, the next bull market lasted about eleven months, and the third, five months.

Shorter-swing stock market movements give even more decided results. Take the New York Stock Exchange Turn Signal, a technical indicator used by *The Markstein Letter*, which I publish (bear in mind that this indicator pictures the past and that past success does not guarantee equal—or any—profits in the future). A trader following this Turn Signal could have made 5. percent "profit" trading the points on this index. Things were as follows:

Long Purchases		Short Sales	
Plus	1.50		
Plus	.59	Plus	4.00
Plus	.50	Plus	5.60
Plus	2.85	Plus	3.29
Plus	8.55	Plus	7.27
Plus	.34	Minus	(1.14)

Long Purchases	Short Sales
Minus (2.95)	Plus .90
Minus (1.46)	Minus (2.57)
Plus 5.44	Plus .68
Minus (1.40)	

There were 13.96 upside profit points, a gain of 23 percent, with 18.63 downside profit points, or 31 percent. A trader "playing" both sides, theoretically selling the index short when a down signal was given, and theoretically buying it on upside indications, could have garnered net 32.59 points, or 54 percent during a time when the index itself moved from a high of 60 to a high of 60—for no gain.

Points to Remember

1. There are both fundamental and technical signposts which tell when a booming stock market is likely to go bust or a sick down market is about to surge upward. Fundamental signs are found in behavior of the economy and of investors themselves. Technical signs include the important Federal Reserve data series "Reserves of Member Banks."

2. An investor selling out close to a top and buying in again close to a bottom is able to make each saved dollar purchase more shares than he sold, thus setting him up, if his judgment is correct, to participate in the new upside movement with a greater number of shares than he had originally possessed and hence greater potential for making his retirement stake grow rapidly.

3. Bull and bear swings come more quickly and last for shorter periods of time than formerly. This intensifies the need for caution and increases the gain opportunities of those who can see the signs of a market turn close to the actual turning point.

Chapter Thirteen
COUNT ON MORE INFLATION

I recently bought a sport coat. It cost 40 percent more than the same brand was selling for a year earlier and 20 percent more than the brand sold for six months previous. Every week my wife has to take a greater number of dollars out of the bank to buy the same quantity of food for the Markstein household. Cars cost more. Gasoline in my town went up by 2¢ per gallon, the third increase in eleven months.

It came as quite a surprise, therefore, to read recently in a government release that consumer prices had not risen. Intrigued, I read on, since Washington's ways with statistics are not always to be taken seriously. Sure enough, *every component of the price index was up. But the Index was unchanged.*

Where but in Washington could that happen?

The point of all this is to say that you will believe in inflation's demise at your peril. It is not dead. It is not going to die, no matter what they do with words or numbers to prove that it is no longer with us. Inflation is the central fact of the American economy today.

Q. How can you be certain inflation is inevitable?

A. Read this, from *U.S. Financial Data,* published by the Federal Reserve Bank of Saint Louis and dated April 19, 1972:

"The nation's money stock, defined as private demand

deposits plus currency in the hands of the public, has expanded at a rapid 8.8 percent annual rate in the past four months and at a 6.3 percent rate in the past year."

Expansion of money supply is thus going on at an increasing rate—faster for four months past than for twelve. *Expand money supply and more dollars are released to chase after the same amount of goods and services. Prices MUST go up in the future if that keeps up.*

Make your plans on the basis that things will cost more in six months than they do now, still more in a year, considerably more in two years.

Q. But government officials say inflation is licked.

A. In a May 12, 1972, speech before the International Banking Conference held in Montreal, Dr. Arthur Burns, Chairman of the Federal Reserve, claimed that U.S. inflation is being licked, and that the Smithsonian Agreement ended "this dangerous trend toward competitive and even antagonistic national economic policies."

His speech came only a month before the floating British pound showed up weaknesses of the Smithsonian Agreement and proved that competitive national policies were not a thing of the past at all.

Said the *Economic Review* of the First National City Bank, June, 1972: "Inflation is the rock on which most forecasts of the U.S. economy have foundered."

Q. Don't greedy union demands bring about inflation?

A. A more important factor is government spending. The unions are easy whipping boys. "They" make inflation. My advisory service, *The Markstein Letter,* along with such economists as the eminent Milton Friedman, has said all along that without monetary increases, inflation could not happen. To quote the Citibank survey again: "Union members account for only one-fourth of the labor force, and this hasn't changed materially over the past decade."

It is less pleasant to face the fact that while the American people demand welfare and carry on war; while government tells unions not to task for more money but raises salaries of city and state employees, hiking social security by big amounts on more than one occasion; most of all while the Federal Reserve increases money supply at a hectic rate while assuring us that things are better, there is no hope for licking inflation.

Q. You mentioned government spending. Explain, please.

A. Few serious economists would deny that the enormous $20 billion federal government deficits—money Washington spent over and above the amount of tax revenue it took in—were a big factor in creating the frightening inflation of the turn of the decade.

Then the government went in for still bigger deficits. On August 10, 1972, I wrote to clients of *The Markstein Letter*:

"Money has increased at an 8.2 percent rate in the past three months . . . [and] velocity has increased substantially in the first half of this year.

"To increased money supply and faster velocity add the staggering Federal budget deficits now being planned. We may be $40 billion in the red this fiscal year, double the Johnson deficits which in large measure produced our present inflation. Wholesale prices spurted 8.4 percent annual rate in July."

Q. Won't price ceilings control inflation?

A. Darryl Francis, the articulate head of the Federal Reserve Bank of Saint Louis, once remarked that imposition of price controls was something like painting a house that is infested with termites. The house will look better after being painted, Mr. Francis said, but the termites will still be there and the damage they do will continue.

Q. Who is at fault?

A. You are. The fellow third from the right in the barbershop line across the street is. The housewife shopping at the corner supermarket is at fault. The welfare recipient who could and should be working is at fault. Everyone who demands services from the government—state, local, county, or federal—is a cause of inflation. We are all at fault.

We're at fault because we have demanded more from our government than it is able to furnish on the funds it receives in taxes. We are at fault for tolerating simultaneously a war and expensive government programs for peace. No criticism of either type of spending is meant here; what is meant is merely that people can't expect governments to do for them more than the governments are financially able to do, and then look to avoid inflation. Politicians begin running for reelection the instant they take office. If their constituencies demand more than they should receive for the tax outgo they are willing to put up, politicians—being realists and not idealists—endeavor to furnish what the electorate demands.

And inflation results. It won't stop.

Q. Then are we all condemned to see our retirement affluence vanish as inflation proceeds inexorably?

A. Not so. Doing something about the problem, and providing means to retire rich despite inflation, is what the preceding chapters of this book have been about.

Points to Remember

1. Inflation is not a temporary problem. It is permanent. Plan on more of it.

2. Inflation is caused primarily by more money chasing the same goods. This occurs when the federal establishment spends more than it takes in, particularly when it runs enormous deficits, and when the Federal Reserve Board expands money supply.

3. Unions make a convenient whipping boy. Their contribution to inflation is realistically small and of no greater degree than the contribution made by businesses which raise prices beyond need in order to counter heightened costs.

Chapter Fourteen

AFTER RETIREMENT—A HIGH INCOME FOR LIFE

"Withdraw my capital? A fine retirement plan that would be!" The speaker, a man in his early sixties, rose to leave the investment counselor's office.

"Wait—you haven't heard it all," said the professional. "I said that under certain circumstances—certainly not all circumstances—a plan of partially withdrawing capital might make your retirement years better ones.

"During the buildup period, when you worked to make your capital grow, you counted on the gains accruing from growth investments to make your total retirement stake bigger. Now that you're retiring, I'm suggesting that you might use some of that accrued growth as income over the years.

"It would certainly be foolish to eat up all of the capital itself. But correctly done, a withdrawal plan can have more money in it at the end of five or ten years of retirement than it had in the beginning. Withdrawal plans aren't any panacea, but they can help. Let's look at them in detail."

You, too, might look at withdrawal plans in detail. They can make retirement years better ones financially —*if done wisely.*

Q. *What is a withdrawal plan?*

A. The following was written for investors by a mutual fund which offers shareholders withdrawal privileges:

"An investor who has acquired shares of the fund that have a value at the current offering price of at least $5,000 may—upon request—have sufficient shares of the fund automatically redeemed at monthly intervals to provide payment to him of $50 or more.

"Under this plan, the investor's shares are deposited with a bank as agent for the shareowner, who signs instructions to the bank specifying the amount of the check to be received each month (or quarter, if desired). With the bank's approval, payments may be revised at any time by the shareholder."

Note this about the plan: If the amount received under a check-each-month plan of the type described above exceeds the amount of the dividends credited to the account, the payments will constitute depletion of capital. As the fund redeems shares for you under this sort of plan, you might find that you have incurred a taxable capital gain if shares were bought at a lower price—or a tax loss, deductible from income under some circumstances, if you paid more for the shares than the cash price at the time they were redeemed.

Q. Can this be done with ordinary shares of stock or only with mutual funds? Would General Motors, for example, redeem or sell some of my shares to give me a steady monthly income if I wished that?

A. They would not. But *you* could do this with any kind of stock, General Motors included.

A sound way would be this: Have your broker hold your shares. Instruct him to pay you out of dividend income where possible and to sell a share now and then to make up the steady income where dividend accrual isn't sufficient. (Whether your broker is willing to do this is a matter you will have to settle in conversation with the firm that buys and sells securities for you.)

Or you can put your dividend checks into a special account. Withdraw from this monthly. If there is not enough money, sell one or more shares of stock, as needed. Be aware that commissions charged by brokerage houses are proportionally larger on small transactions such as this than when bigger, round-lot amounts are involved.

Q. My retirement capital is in income-producing real estate. What then?

A. It is not as easy to sell off a chunk of property as a share of stock. But you can do it under some circumstances, such as where a large number of small parcels or several units of a condominium are involved.

Q. Won't I eventually eat up all of my capital this way and so find that the stake I accumulated to make my retirement years happy won't be around to do its job?

A. This is a danger. It has been stressed that a withdrawal plan is not something to enter into lightly or one that every retiree should practice.

Q. Is the plan workable with any kind of stock?

A. Growth-oriented investments typically pay lower percentage yields, holding out the hope of capital gains. It's best to use a withdrawal plan in connection with such growth securities. When a plan operates as it is expected to—and you can't count upon this with certainty—the stock, or mutual fund shares which are invested in growth securities, will appreciate at least to the degree of the withdrawal; hopefully, even faster. Past performance is no guarantee of future results, yet it is still interesting to see how withdrawal would have worked in a past case of one performance-oriented mutual fund:

Had an investor started with $10,000 in fund shares (immediately reduced to $9,200 by the cost of commissions), plowing back capital gains distributions, withdrawing a steady $50 per month during ten years, and using capital itself when dividend income was not enough, he would have withdrawn $6,000 in both classifications over the decade. At the end of that time, his $10,000 would *still* have grown to $29,682!

Q. Would this be workable with funds accumulated under a Keogh plan for the self-employed?

A. After retirement, yes. You would not want to generate added income before retirement since the purpose of your Keogh setup is to defer today's income until a later date. Consult your CPA or other advisor about the tax angles.

Q. If I withdraw shares during a period when the stock market is in trouble, such as happened in 1969 and 1970, won't I lose money?

A. You will. That is only one of many possible complications to a withdrawal plan. You should enter one cautiously and only after securing professional advice based upon individual needs and wants.

Q. Are dual funds good vehicles for this sort of retirement plan?

A. Dual funds have two components. The "capital" investors receive all gains when the portfolio appreciates (and absorb capital losses when it depreciates), while "income" investors receive all dividends from both components. But remember that additions to capital value accrue to capital shares; thus if you sell income shares, you're largely deprived of the hope that growing value will make up your loss.

Q. Other than withdrawal plans, what high-income investments are available with safety of income and principal?

A. There are classes of government securities which fit this. In regard to the following (the quoted part of which has been reprinted from *The Markstein Letter*) bear in mind that interest rates are those pertaining in mid-1972 and that these might be lower or higher by the time you read this, depending upon how the trends of the money market go:

1. " 'Passthroughs' of Ginnie Mae are an interesting investment idea. If you have capital enough to meet minimum investment, the Letter recommends you give them serious attention.

"Ginnie Mae is the Government National Mortgage Association. People call it 'Ginnie Mae' from its initials. The good thing about Ginnie Mae securities is the high interest, running about 7 percent, which is guaranteed by the government as to both interest and principal. The bad thing is that you can't buy Ginnie Mae passthroughs in small packages; $25,000 is about the smallest ante you can put up to enter that game.

"Money raised by sale of Ginnie Mae's guaranteed certificates is used to finance mortgages. Ginnie Mae's guarantees are backed by full faith and credit of the Federal establishment.

"Bit outfits sell parts of the pools they have purchased –thereby 'passing through' the deal to investors who can thus purchase parts of an investment medium originally designed for big institutional operators on the order of pension trusts."

86   AFTER RETIREMENT—A HIGH INCOME FOR LIFE

2. Another income-producer is a type of bond from the U.S. Small Business Administration. This brings a tremendous 6.9-percent return.

Small Business Investment Corporations are chartered to invest money in risky ventures that ordinary lenders might not be able to touch. They enjoy tax and other advantages as incentive to do this. The SBICs come under federal jurisdiction of the Small Business Administration. Part of its job is to assure liquidity of the local SBICs so they can continue their function of furnishing capital to burgeoning new ventures, and to assure opportunity and access to capital for firms that might not otherwise have the opportunity to become tomorrow's GMs, GEs, and IBMs.

A typical 1972 SBA recently issued was $38.5 million ten-year debentures to help finance SBICs. These are fully guaranteed. Carrying a 7.0 percent coupon, they were peddled at 101.07 percent to yield the public 6.9 percent—a very sizable return on a class of security carrying only the risk that the U.S. government might cease to exist in the next decade, or might repudiate its guarantees. Without either of those unlikely happenings, investors holding the debentures cannot lose dollar value of their principal and are rewarded with a high interest yield for ten years. Proceeds went to help forty-nine Small Business Investment Corporations in twenty-two states.

3. You can get 6-percent to 7-percent income from other debt instruments that can be considered semigovernment obligations.

These juicy yields are found in notes, bonds, debentures of such agencies as the Federal National Mortgage Association, Federal Home Loan Bank, and World Bank. Although the latter is no part of the U.S. government, it

s inconceivable that the United States would permit a
default on its bonds.

Typical yields in mid-1972 were:
FNMA 4½'s due February, 1977 ....6.06%
FNMA 7¼'s due June, 1981 ....6.66%
Federal Home Loan 6.6's, November, 1981 ......6.67%
Federal Land Bank 4⅛'s, February, 1973 ....6.16%
Federal Land Bank 5⅝'s, April, 1978 ....6.19%
World Bank 4½'s, February, 1990 ....7.07%
World Bank 6⅞'s, October, 1994 ....7.29%

These were selected because they sell at or below par,
expressed as 100 but actually $1,000 since bonds are
issued in that denomination. If you buy a bond with a
lower face yield, paying less than par to achieve higher
income, you get a built-in capital gain when it is redeemed at full value.

Points to Remember

1. The time to make capital grow is before retirement,
when you want to accumulate the largest possible stake.
Then the portfolio should be changed to bring in great-
est income after retirement.

2. One way to bring in more income is through withdrawal plans. These permit the planner to obtain a predetermined income regardless of prevailing yield conditions. A danger is that, unless wisely carried out, a
withdrawal plan can deplete capital.

3. Certain kinds of government and semigovernment
securities bring in a high return with guarantees of
income and principal.